Jamie Fleeman's Country Cookbook

Traditional Recipes from the North East of Scotland

Collected by
Margaret Hamilton

Illustrated by
Mairi Hedderwick

© Famedram Publ
Gartocharn

© Famedram Publishers Limited
Printed by Famedram Publishers Limited, Gartocharn, Scotland.

Contents

Introduction

AS MOST Buchan folk will know, Jamie Fleeman was the Laird of Udny's Fool. He lived in the eighteenth century and was well known for his pithy wit. One of his most quoted sayings — "I'm the Laird of Udny's Feel". Wha's feel are ye?"

It is ironic really that Fleeman's name should be linked with either the Laird of Udny or a kitchen. He died in dire poverty without obvious support from his patron. Apparently he was none too keen on the cooks of the various households in which he was employed. He had pretty strong prejudices against certain groups of people which included factors as well as cooks — "Plant it wi' factors, they thrive in every place". And cooks gave him a hard time according to Pratt's *The Life and Death of Jamie Fleeman* — "they would give him nothing to eat unless he kept plenty of peats and water about their hands", constantly tormenting him with their cries 'Peats, peats, Fleeman' and 'Water, water, Fleeman'.

Now there is a shop in Udny Green, Aberdeenshire

· Jamie Fleeman's ·

named after him and its main activity is the sale of local produce such as smoked salmon pâté, sea trout dishes, shortbread, Dundee cake, tablet, jams and jellies. Most of the preparation and cooking of these is done in the Udny Castle kitchen. The dining room at the Castle is still known as Jamie Fleeman's Kitchen.

This book is not just a book of recipes of those times necessarily, but rather of just good old-fashioned dishes which have stood the test of time and are still very much in use today. They reflect a plainness and economy of cooking — "nane o' ye're fancy stuff here!" Often one dish will provide meals for two or three days.

Look for for any of the old commercial hotel type of establishment still surviving in parts of the north-east, which serve home-made soup of the day with mince and mealies and a comforting hot pudding. Sadly a lot of them have gone, with scampi and chips and fast food counters in their place.

Thanks are due to a number of people who have given their special recipes for this book and most principally to Mrs Paterson, the cook for Jamie Fleeman's Country Kitchen. Her know-how really comes into its own in the next book *Jamie Fleeman's Book of Hearty Breakfasts and High Teas* — as she is a Scottish home-baker supreme!

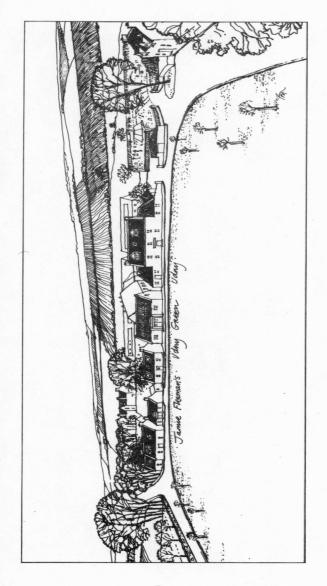

Jamie Freeman's. Wany Green. Wany.

WINTER SOUPS

Barley Soup

2 lbs shin of beef
4 oz pearl barley
Bunch of parsley stalks
4 onions, chopped
6 potatoes, chopped
3 - 4 quarts water
Chopped parsley, salt and pepper

Barley Soup

Put all ingredients in large pan and simmer gently for about 3 hours. Remove parsley stalks and serve with chopped parsley. Adjust seasoning.

Liver Soup

8 oz liver
3 potatoes, 1 onion, sliced
3 carrots, 1 small turnip, grated
Thyme, salt and pepper

Cut liver into small dice and put into pan with 3 pints cold water. Add vegetables and bring to boil. Season with salt and pepper and a little thyme. Simmer 2 - 3 hours.

Kail Brose

2 heads of curly kail
4 oz oatmeal
½ pint beef stock
A little cream or top of the milk
Salt and pepper

Boil kail and sieve or chop very finely. Put back in pan and sprinkle in oatmeal. Add boiling stock. Stir well, season and add cream or milk. Serve with oatcakes and butter.

Crofter Broth

1½ pints chicken stock
6 oz streaky bacon
2 leeks
2 potatoes, sliced
2 carrots, diced
3 oz cabbage, finely shredded
Thyme, parsley
Salt and pepper

Chop bacon into small dice. Clean and slice leeks. Put bacon into heavy saucepan and cook over moderate heat until it begins to colour, stirring frequently. Add leeks and potatoes. Cover with buttered greaseproof paper and lid and sweat for 10 minutes. Remove paper and add carrots and cabbage. Stir in stock and seasoning and cover with lid. Cook for approximately 20 minutes over low heat until cabbage is soft.

Cock-a-Leekie

1 boiling fowl
10 – 12 leeks
2 quarts water
Salt and pepper, chopped parsley
12 prunes

Wash and slice leeks into 1 inch lengths, including green part. Put half the leeks into pan with boiling fowl. Add water and seasoning and bring to boil. Simmer for 1½ hours and add the rest of the leeks. Cook for another 30 minutes. Lift out chicken and save for main dish. Skim the soup well and add prunes. Simmer for 30 minutes and serve with chopped parsley scattered over the top.

Winter Pea Soup

1 pint split peas
1 onion, 1 carrot, 1 leek
1 ham or bacon bone
1 oz butter
1 teaspoon sugar
2 sprigs of mint
1 quart water

Soak peas overnight. Chop vegetables and sweat in butter with lid on pan for a few minutes. Add bone (or two rashers of bacon), soaked peas, sugar and mint. Add water and bring to boil. Simmer until tender — 1 - 1½ hours. Remove bone and mint and put peas through Mouli. Reheat, season and add a little cream or top of milk if desired. Very good served with snippets of fried bread.

Oatmeal Vegetable Soup

1 large onion
2 carrots, diced
2 thick slices of turnip, diced
2 leeks, thinly sliced
1 oz medium oatmeal
1 pint stock
¾ pint milk
Chopped parsley, salt and pepper

Put vegetables into a heavy pan and toss in a little fat until fat is absorbed. Put on lid and sweat for 10 minutes. Add oatmeal and fry with vegetables for a few minutes. Season, add stock and simmer for 45 minutes. Add heated milk and scatter over chopped parsley before serving.

Chicken Broth with Dumplings

1 old boiling fowl
2 onions
2 carrots
1 leek
1 stalk celery
A small bunch of herbs (bay leaf, parsley, thyme etc.)
12 peppercorns
1 blade of mace
3 - 4 pints water
Salt

Put all ingredients into pan and bring to boil. Simmer for about 3 hours and strain. Cool and remove all fat. Dice all the best of chicken meat. Add to strained soup and reheat. Drop dumplings into soup and boil for 5 minutes before serving. Adjust seasoning.

Suet Dumplings

8 oz self-raising flour
3 oz shredded suet
1 teaspoon salt
Chopped parsley
Approximately ¼ pint water

Mix dry ingredients and add water gradually. Do not let the dough get too wet. Form into tiny balls. Roll in seasoned flour.

Chestnut and Potato Soup

1 lb chestnuts
2 lbs potatoes, 2 carrots, 1 large onion
2 oz butter, ¼ pint hot milk
Mixed herbs, salt and pepper

Wash chestnuts, cut a small piece of skin from each and boil for 45 minutes until soft. Skin chestnuts when warm and chop up. Put 2 quarts water into heavy pan and bring to boil. Chop vegetables into dice. Put into pan with chestnuts. Season and simmer for 2 hours. Adjust seasoning, add chopped parsley and milk.

Scotch Broth

"In Aberdeen at dinner, Dr Johnson ate several plates of scotch broth, with barley and peas in it, and seemed very fond of the dish. I said 'you never ate it before?' — Johnson, 'No Sir: but I don't care how soon I eat it again'." Boswell: *Journal of a Tour to the Hebrides with Samuel Johnson (1786)*

Dr. Johnson & Scotch Broth
— & Mr. Boswell.

1 - 2 lbs neck or scrag end of mutton or lamb
1 cup broth mix or pearl barley and dried pulses
1 stalk celery
1 slice turnip
1 carrot
1 onion
1 large leek
3 - 4 pints water
Chopped parsley, salt and pepper

Cut mutton up and put into water. Bring to boil and skim. Add broth mix and simmer for about an hour. Cut vegetables into small dice and continue cooking broth for another hour or so. Remove mutton bones and slice off some good pieces and return to pot. Skim again if necessary, adjust seasoning and add chopped parsley.

Cullen Skink

1 smoked haddock
6 oz mashed potatoes
1 onion, sliced
1 oz butter
1 pint milk
Chopped parsley, salt and pepper

Place haddock and onion in pan with sufficient cold water to cover. Bring to the boil and simmer until cooked, approximately 10 minutes. Lift out fish and remove skin and bones. Flake flesh. Return skin and bones to pan and simmer in liquid with onions for 30 minutes. Strain and return to rinsed out pan. Boil milk in another pan and add to fish stock. Add flaked fish and enough mashed potatoes to give a smooth consistency. Add butter in small pieces, pepper and a little more salt if necessary. Sprinkle over chopped parsley and serve very hot with triangles of dry toast.

Lentil Soup

1 pint lentils
1 onion
1 bacon bone
3 pints water
Chopped mint
Salt

Pick over lentils and rinse. Put into pan with sliced onion, bacon bone, water and salt. Bring to boil and simmer until lentils are really soft. Put through a fine Mouli and if too thick, thin down with some vegetable stock or potato water. Reheat, adjust seasoning and scatter over chopped mint. Diced crisply fried bacon on the top is a good addition.

SUMMER SOUPS

Nettle Kail

· Nettle Kail ·

Kail was the common name for broth and usually meant the whole dinner. From **Jamieson**, *Dictionary of the Scottish Language* — "Hence, in giving a friendly invitation to dinner, it is common to say 'Will you come and tak' your kail' wi' me?'"

Nettles are a good substitute for spinach in early spring and once had the reputation for purifying the blood, clearing the complexion and in general ensuring good health. Shrove Tuesday was traditionally the occasion for a nettle kail supper.

Nettles
1 cup oatmeal, 1 onion, finely chopped
1 chicken or 2 pints chicken stock
a little cream, chopped mint, salt and pepper

Gather young nettles in the early morning before the sun gets to them. Strip off leaves and wash in salted water. Chop up the larger leaves. Put chicken into large pot with 2 quarts cold water. Bring to boil and add nettles and oatmeal, stirring well. Add salt and onion. Simmer until bird is tender. Lift out and save for main dish of the meal. Stir cream or sour cream into soup and scatter over with freshly chopped mint. Serve with oatcakes and butter.

Broad Bean Soup

This is a good way of using beans when they are large and past their best. If the skins look very tough remove them before cooking.

1 lb broad beans
1 onion, chopped
1 quart chicken or ham stock
1 oz butter
A little cream or top of the milk
2 sprigs savory, salt and pepper

Melt butter in pan and soften onion. Add beans and stir over heat for a few minutes. Add stock, savory and seasoning. Bring to boil and simmer for 30 minutes. Put through Mouli. Reheat and add cream or milk.

Newburgh Mussels Soup

2 quarts mussels
1 small onion, finely chopped
1 stick celery
A bunch of herbs (bay leaf, thyme and parsley stalks)
1 glass white wine
½ pint water or fish stock
Chopped parsley and freshly ground black pepper

Wash and scrub mussels thoroughly. Put into large pan with onion, herbs and liquid. Cover and bring to the boil shaking the pan occasionally. Simmer for a few minutes. Discard any mussels which haven't opened. Pour off liquid into saucepan. Reboil and thicken, if desired, with a little arrowroot or kneaded butter. Add parsley. Put mussels into soup tureen, remove top shells and pour over soup.

Summer Soup

1 heart savoy cabbage, 1 lettuce, shredded
2 tomatoes, 2 leeks, 2 potatoes, chopped
8 oz green beans, 8 oz shelled peas
2 oz butter, 2 pints water, ½ pint milk
Chopped mint, salt and pepper

Put vegetables in a heavy pan. Add butter, water and seasoning and bring to boil. Simmer gently until potatoes are tender. Add milk and heat through gently before serving.

· Lettuce Soup ·

Cream of Lettuce Soup

This is a good way of using up lettuces when there are too many ready at once!

2 or 3 lettuces
1 onion, finely chopped
1 oz butter, 1 oz flour
1½ pints milk or light stock with cream added later
Chopped mint, salt and pepper

Shred the lettuce. Melt butter and add lettuce and onion. Cook gently for a few minutes. Add flour and milk or stock. Season and simmer for 20 minutes. Put through fine sieve and reheat. Scatter over chopped mint and serve with fried croutons.

Fresh Green Pea Soup

1 lettuce and a handful of spinach leaves
3 - 4 young leeks, green part only
1 quart large shelled peas
1 cup small fresh green peas
1 teaspoon sugar, 2 oz butter, salt and pepper
1 quart light stock or water

Wash the vegetables and shred finely. Put these with large peas into pan with sugar, butter, salt and pepper. Sweat for a few minutes with the lid on. Add stock and bring to boil. Simmer for 30 - 40 minutes and put through Mouli or fine sieve. Cook small green peas in salted water until tender. Reheat soup and serve in tureen with small green peas and chopped mint.

Cream of Carrot Soup

1½ lbs carrots, 1 onion, 1 potato, sliced
2 oz butter
1 pint chicken stock or water
½ pint creamy milk
chopped wild garlic
1 yolk of egg
¼ pint cream
Salt and pepper

Melt butter in pan and add carrots, onion and garlic. Season and sweat with lid on for 10 minutes. Add potato and stir over heat for a few moments. Add stock and milk. Bring to boil and simmer gently for about 30 minutes. Put through Mouli or sieve. Mix cream and egg yolk together and add gradually to soup. Stir over heat until the soup thickens without boiling.

Sorrel Soup

4 handfuls sorrel leaves
1 onion, sliced
1 oz butter
¾ oz flour
1½ pints beef or ham stock
½ pint milk, warmed
Chopped chives, salt and pepper
A sqeeze of lemon juice
A little cream, lightly whipped

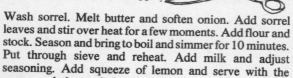

Wash sorrel. Melt butter and soften onion. Add sorrel leaves and stir over heat for a few moments. Add flour and stock. Season and bring to boil and simmer for 10 minutes. Put through sieve and reheat. Add milk and adjust seasoning. Add squeeze of lemon and serve with the cream and chopped chives on top.

FISH DISHES

MacDuff Prawns.

Potted Macduff Prawns

2 lbs prawns
4 oz butter
1 teaspoon ground mace
1 tablespoon chopped mixed herbs
Ground black pepper and cayenne pepper

Clarify butter by melting gently in saucepan. When it is frothing before changing colour, pour off, leaving sediment behind. Peel prawns leaving one each serving for decoration. Put in frying pan with some of the butter and fry quickly adding herbs, spices and seasoning. Fill into little china pots or moulds. Press down and pour over more butter to completely cover the prawns. Keep in cold place for several hours. Turn out onto plates and surround with lettuce hearts and quartered lemons. Serve with hot toast and butter.

Soused Herrings

4 herrings
¾ pint malt vinegar and water mixed
1 bay leaf, 2 cloves, 8 peppercorns, a blade of mace
1 medium onion, sliced,
salt and freshly ground black pepper

Split and fillet herrings. Roll up from head to tail and place in fireproof dish. Heat vinegar with all the spices and seasoning and allow to cool. Pour over herrings and bake in a low oven for about an hour.

Marinated Kippers

2 kipper fillets per person
French dressing made with lemon or vinegar
1 onion, finely chopped, freshly ground black pepper

Skin fillets. Cut them across in thin strips. Make French dressing in usual way and add chopped onion. Lay fish in deep dish or bowl and cover with dressing. Chill for several hours or overnight. Serve with buttered brown bread.

Fried Plaice with Anchovy Sauce

4 fillets of plaice
1 egg
Fresh white breadcrumbs
Salt and pepper
½ pint white or bechamel sauce
1½ tablespoons of anchovy essence

Wash and dry plaice fillets. Season and cover with breadcrumbs. Press well in. Fry in oil and butter until light golden on both sides. Add anchovy essence to white sauce and serve separately.

Salmon or Smoked Haddock Kedgeree

8 oz cooked fish, flaked
2 hard boiled eggs
1 small onion, finely chopped
3 oz butter
8 oz rice
A squeeze of lemon, a little cream
Chopped parsley, salt and ground black pepper

Boil rice in plenty of boiling salted water. Drain thoroughly. Soften onion in butter without browning. Add flaked fish, chopped hard boiled eggs and rice. Stir gently with a fork until hot. Add parsley, lemon juice, salt and ground black pepper. At the last minute stir in cream.

Aberdeen Fish Pie

1 lb cooked flaked fish (mixed smoked haddock, ling or
cod is best)
1½ lbs mashed potatoes
2 hard boiled eggs
3 tomatoes, skinned, pipped and chopped
¾ pint of creamy white or bechamel sauce
Chopped parsley
Salt and freshly ground black pepper

Make the sauce. This can be made with the milk in which the fish has been previously cooked. Lay the fish in a buttered pie dish with quartered hard boiled eggs and chopped tomatoes. Sprinkle over each layer with chopped parsley, salt and ground pepper. Pour over sauce and then top with mashed potatoes. Mark top with fork and dot over with pieces of butter. Bake in hot oven until crisp and brown on top.

East Coast Flan

8 oz kipper fillets, flaked
2 eggs, 4 oz cheese, ¼ pint milk
4 oz shortcrust pastry
Freshly ground black pepper

· *East Coast Flan* ·

Roll out pastry and line an 8 inch flan tin. Beat the eggs, add milk and grated cheese. Add flaked kipper and pepper. Pour into flan case and bake in moderately hot oven for 30 - 40 minutes.

Herring and Oatmeal Pie

1 lb fresh herrings
2 tablespoons vinegar, 2 tablespoons seasoned flour
2 leeks, sliced, 1 lb potatoes chopped
2 oz fat, 4 oz oatmeal, 4 oz flour

Clean, bone and split herrings. Dip in vinegar and then into seasoned flour. Roll up herrings and place in pie dish. Add leeks and potatoes to dish and add enough water to come half way up dish. Rub fat into oatmeal and flour. Mix with a little cold water to form a stiff paste. Roll out on floured board and cover dish. Bake for about 1 hour in a moderate oven.

Finnan Haddie

1 large smoked haddock
½ pint milk
¼ pint water
1 oz butter
Freshly ground black pepper

Cover fish with milk and water in oven dish. Poach with lid on or cover with buttered paper. Lift out and remove backbone, fins and tail. Divide into two portions. Keep warm while poaching eggs in the same milk. Place egg on each portion of haddock and pour over milk. Sprinkle with black pepper and dot over pieces of butter. Serve with hot toast and butter.

· Finnan Haddie ·

Fishcakes

Equal parts of cooked flaked fish (salmon, smoked
*   haddock or white fish) and mashed potatoes*
Chopped parsley
1 egg
1 oz butter, seasoning
Egg and breadcrumbs

Mix potatoes and fish. Season well. Add butter, beaten egg and chopped parsley. Spread on a plate and chill thoroughly. Shape on floured board into flat cakes. Egg and breadcrumb and fry in shallow fat. Serve with quartered lemons.

Herrings in Oatmeal

2 herrings per person
Oatmeal
Salt and pepper
Oil and butter for frying

Clean and prepare fish. Split open and remove backbone. Season with salt and pepper. Roll fish in oatmeal, pressing well into flesh to make it stick. Heat butter and oil and fry split side down first. When golden brown on both sides, drain on kitchen paper and serve with sprigs of parsley and quartered lemons.

Skate with Black Butter

1½ - 2 lbs wing of skate
1 onion, sliced
Parsley stalks, 1 bay leaf
3 tablespoons vinegar
Salt and pepper

Black Butter

3 oz butter
1 tablespoon wine vinegar
1 dessertspoon capers, chopped parsley

Wash the skate thoroughly in salted water. Put in fireproof dish and cover with water. Add sliced onion, parsley stalks, bay leaf, seasoning and vinegar. Poach in oven for about 30 minutes. Lift out skate and carefully take skin away from both sides. Place on hot serving dish. Put butter in saucepan and heat quickly until it foams and begins to brown. Pour over the fish. Add vinegar to pan and heat. Sprinkle fish with parsley and capers and pour over vinegar.

Salmon Pie

1 lb cooked salmon, broken in large pieces
¾ pint bechamel or cream sauce
2 hard boiled eggs, quartered
A squeeze of lemon juice
Copped parsley
Salt and freshly ground black pepper
Flaky or shortcrust pastry
1 egg, beaten

Line a shallow round pie dish with pastry. Add salmon
and eggs to sauce. Season well and add squeeze of lemon
juice and chopped parsley. Cool and fill into prepared pie
dish. Cover with pastry lid and decorate with pastry leaves
etc. Brush over with beaten egg. Bake in hot oven for 20 -
30 minutes until pastry is well risen and golden brown.

Grilled Salmon Steaks with Herb Butter

1 salmon steak per person
Softened butter
Chopped herbs, salt and pepper
Extra butter

Cut salmon into 1½ inch steaks. Season on both sides.
Work chopped herbs (parsley, chives and thyme) into
butter and spread over top side. Cook under very hot grill
for 3 - 4 minutes. Turn over and spread with herb butter.
Grill again for 3 - 4 minutes. Pour juices from grill pan
into saucepan and add extra butter. Serve steaks with
quartered lemons and hand hot herb butter separately.

Baked Ythan Sea Trout.

Baked Ythan Sea Trout

1 sea trout, 2 - 3 lbs
2 tablespoons mixed chopped herbs
2 oz butter
1 glass white wine or juice of 1 lemon
1 dessertspoon cream
Rough sea salt and freshly ground black pepper
1 dessertspoon arrowroot

Clean sea trout and dry. Place on large piece of buttered foil. Cream 1 oz of the butter with half the herbs and stuff cavity. Spread the rest of the softened butter all over fish and sprinkle with salt and pepper. Pour over wine or lemon juice and fold up foil into a loose parcel. Place in roasting tin and cook in moderate oven for 35 - 45 minutes. Lift out fish, skin and place on ashet to keep warm. Put all juices from foil parcel into saucepan and reheat. Mix arrowroot to a paste with a very little water. Add to fish juices and stir over heat until slightly thickened. Add rest of chopped herbs and cream. Pour a little of this sauce over fish and serve the rest in a sauceboat.

Poached Cod with Egg Sauce

2 cod fillets
½ pint milk
1 bay leaf
1 oz butter
¾ oz flour
2 hard boiled eggs, chopped
Chopped parsley
Salt and pepper

Wash and dry cod fillets. Lay in buttered fireproof dish and pour over milk barely to cover. Add bay leaf, cover with a piece of buttered paper and poach in oven for about 20 minutes. Lift out fish and keep warm. Melt butter in saucepan, add flour, pour on milk in which fish has cooked and stir until boiling. Add chopped hard-boiled eggs, parsley, salt and pepper and pour over fish.

MAIN DISHES

Haggis, Neeps & Tatties with Atholl Brose.

Haggis, Neeps and Tatties with Atholl Brose

Scotland's great national dish and here is a recipe from an old farm kitchen handed down over the years and still in regular use today. Vegetarians are advised to skip this one. It is traditional to wash the haggis down with liberal amounts of Atholl Brose or a single malt whisky from the local distillery.

1 mutton paunch
Heart, lungs and liver of sheep
2 onions, finely chopped. 6 oz toasted oatmeal
1 lb beef suet, shredded. ¾ pint strong stock
Salt, white and cayenne pepper, nutmeg

Wash the paunch and turn inside out. Boil the heart, lungs and liver until tender. When cool, chop the meat finely and grate the liver. Spread the chopped mixture out and season with salt, peppers and nutmeg. Add the other ingredients and mix together with stock. Fill paunch, leaving plenty of room for the oatmeal to swell. Sew up and prick over with a needle. Boil for about 3 hours and serve with neeps and tatties and a glass of Atholl Brose.

Neeps and Tatties

1 turnip, 2 lbs potatoes
2 oz butter and a little milk, salt and pepper

Peel and roughly chop turnip. Boil until tender, about 1 hour. Drain off water thoroughly. Mash, add 1 oz butter and season highly with salt and pepper. Do likewise to boiled potatoes adding a little milk as well.

Atholl Brose

Mix equal quantities of the strained liquid obtained by soaking oatmeal in water for at least 30 minutes and malt whisky. Add heather honey and stir until thoroughly blended.

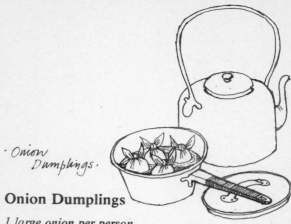

Onion Dumplings

Onion Dumplings

1 large onion per person
1 dessertspoon well-seasoned mince per onion
Plain suet crust

Peel onions and cut them across. Take out hearts and replace with mince. Put halves together and wrap up in suet crust. (See recipe for steak and kidney pudding). Tie each in a little cloth, plunge into boiling water and boil steadily for 1½ – 2 hours according to the size of dumplings.

Stovies

8 oz cooked lamb or beef, roughly chopped
2½ lbs potatoes, 3 large onions, sliced
2 oz beef dripping or roast fat
½ pint gravy or stock, salt and pepper

Melt dripping in thick-bottomed pan. Put in a layer of onions and then a layer of potatoes. Continue, adding salt and pepper to each layer. Cover and cook gently for about 30 minutes. Add gravy or stock and chopped meat. Stir through and cook for another 20 - 30 minutes. Adjust seasoning.

Clapshot

1 lb potatoes
1 lb turnip
2 dessertspoon chopped chives
1 oz butter or beef dripping
Salt and pepper
Gravy
Croutons of fried bread

Clapshot

Boil potatoes and turnip separately. Drain and mash well together. Add the other ingredients. If chives are not available, add some finely chopped onion softened in butter. Serve very hot piled up in the centre of a hot dish, garnished with fried croûtons and pour round good gravy or brown sauce. Clapshot is often served with mince or cold meat.

Skirlie

1 cup medium oatmeal
1 onion, finely chopped
2 tablespoons dripping or 2 oz shredded suet
Salt and pepper

Melt fat in hot frying pan and add onions. Fry until golden brown. Stir in oatmeal and cook lightly for 5 - 10 minutes. Season well and serve piping hot with mashed potatoes.

Mince and Mealies

1 lb minced beef
1 oz roast fat or dripping
1 small onion, finely chopped
½ carrot, finely diced
½ pint meat gravy or stock
½ oz flour
2 white "mealie puddings"

Melt fat in stewpan and brown meat, onion and carrot over brisk heat for a few minutes, keeping turning and stirring. Add flour and gravy or stock. Cook covered for 40 minutes and then drop in mealies. Cook for another 20 minutes. The puddings may burst but this doesn't matter and will only improve the flavour of the mince.

Oxtail Stew

1 oxtail
1 onion, 1 carrot
1 stick of celery, sliced
2 oz pearl barley
1 small bunch of herbs
Chopped parsley
Salt and pepper

Divide oxtails and wash. Put them into stewpan with water to cover. Add salt and bring to boil. Remove scum and add barley and vegetables. Cook on top of stove or in the oven for about 2 hours. Take out bunch of herbs and skim. Check seasoning and scatter over chopped parsley.

Mealie Puddings

Mealie Puddings

This is a recipe from another Udny farmhouse kitchen renowned in the area as the best producer of home-made "mealie puddins".

1 lb beef suet
¾ lb onions, finely chopped
2 lbs toasted oatmeal
1 dessertspoon salt and ½ teaspoon pepper
Pudding skins

Get the skins from a butcher and ask for the suet to be minced or chopped. This is according to taste. Wash pudding skins and turn inside out. Toast oatmeal gently in oven on a baking tray for 5 minutes. Mix suet with onions, add oatmeal and salt and pepper and mix well. Fill into skins not filling too full so as to leave room for the oatmeal to swell. Divide and tie with string every 5 inches or so. Boil for 10 minutes.

Lentil Cakes

1 lb red lentils
8 oz mashed potatoes
1 onion, finely chopped
1 tablespoon chopped parsley
Salt and pepper
1 egg, beaten
Browned crumbs or medium oatmeal

Boil the lentils until mushy and drain. Soften onion in a little butter and add to lentils with mashed potato. Season well, add parsley and spread on plate until cool. Form into cakes and dip in beaten egg. Coat with browned crumbs or oatmeal and fry on both sides until brown and crisp. Serve with a sharp fresh tomato sauce or spicy brown sauce. Also delicious cold, served with salad.

Tripe and Onions

2 lb tripe
6 large onions, sliced
1 oz butter or dripping
½ pint stock or water
1 oz butter and 1 oz flour
Chopped parsley,
Salt and pepper

Melt butter or dripping in stewpan. Soften onions. Cut tripe into large squares or strips. Add to onions and add salt and lots of pepper. Barely cover with stock or water. Cook gently for about 1 hour. Lift out tripe and arrange in clean dish. Make roux with butter and flour and pour on liquid from pan. Stir until smooth and pour over tripe. Scatter over chopped parsley and serve with made mustard.

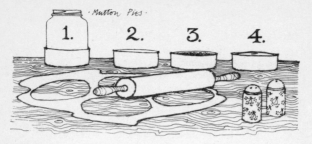

Mutton Pies

1 lb mutton or lamb from shoulder
1 onion, finely chopped
1 teaspoon Worcestershire sauce
A pinch of ground mace
A little kneaded butter and flour or cornflour
Chopped parsley, salt and pepper

Chop mutton or lamb roughly, removing all fat. Put in pan with onion and barely cover with water. Add salt and pepper. Cover and cook gently for about 30 minutes. Thicken slightly with kneaded butter and flour or a little cornflour. Add chopped parsley, Worcestershire sauce and mace. Season highly.

Hot Water Crust

1 lb flour
A pinch of salt
4 oz dripping or roast fat
1 egg, beaten
¼ pint water, approx.

Put fat and water into pan and bring to boil. Pour immediately on to sifted flour and salt in a bowl. Mix and turn onto floured board. Knead quickly and set aside about a third of the paste for the lids. Roll out and mould round and up about 2½ inches of a jam jar.

Put filling into moulds and then roll out rest of pastry. Dampen edges and pinch the lids on. Make ½ inch slit on centre of each pie, brush all over with beaten egg and set on baking tray. Put in hot oven for about 20 minutes.

Boiled Beef and Dumplings

4 - 5 lb silverside or rump of beef
5 onions
5 carrots, cut in quarters lengthways
1 turnip, cut in thick slices
1 bay leaf, sprig of thyme and some parsley stalks
1 onion stuck with a clove
8 peppercorns

Put beef into large pan and cover well with water. Bring slowly to boil, skimming frequently. Add herbs, pepper-corns and onion stuck with a clove. Simmer for 1 - 2 hours. Remove herbs and onion and skim. Add the vegetables and cook for another hour. Drop in dumplings and simmer for a further 20 minutes with the pan covered. Serve the beef on ashet surrounded with the vegetables and dumplings. Serve some of the soup separately in a sauce-boat.

Dumplings

8 oz self-raising flour
4 oz shredded suet
A pinch of salt, pepper and thyme
A little water

Sift flour with salt and add suet. Add thyme, salt and pepper. Moisten with water and make a light dough. Divide into small pieces and roll between the palms of the hands into little balls. When cooked lift out from stock with a perforated spoon or skimmer.

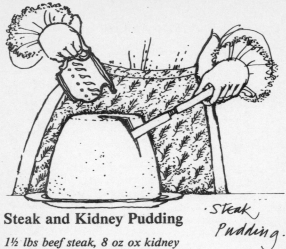

Steak and Kidney Pudding

Steak Pudding.

1½ lbs beef steak, 8 oz ox kidney
1 small onion, finely chopped
1 dessertspoon mixed herbs, finely chopped
Seasoned flour, salt and pepper

Suet Crust

1 lb self-raising flour, a pinch of salt
8 oz shredded suet, approximately ½ pint water

Sift flour with salt and rub in suet lightly. Mix to a soft dough with water. Cut off two-thirds of paste and roll out on floured board to a round about 1 inch thick. Dust with flour and fold in two. Pull out ends a little and shape into a sort of bag to line a greased pudding basin. Cut steak into ½ inch squares and cut kidney into pieces. Roll in seasoned flour and arrange in basin in layers with chopped onion and herbs. Add water till basin is three parts full. Roll out remaining paste and cover over rim of basin, pressing well round edges. Trim and tie cloth or round of greaseproof paper over the top. Put basin into a large pan and fill up half way with boiling water. Boil steadily for about 3 hours topping up with boiling water from time to time. Have a jug with a little boiling hot stock or water when serving so as when the first slice is cut this can be added to the juices in the pudding.

Boiled Gigot with Caper Sauce

1 leg of lamb
1 large onion, 2 carrots
1 turnip, sliced
1 bunch of mixed herbs, salt and pepper

Caper Sauce
1 oz butter, 1 oz flour
½ pint lamb stock
½ teaspoon made mustard, salt and pepper
1 tablespoon capers, a little cream

Put lamb into large pan and cover with water. Bring to boil and simmer for 30 minutes. Skim and add vegetables and herbs. Season and simmer for about 1½ hours. Lift out meat and put on ashet. Chop vegetables and arrange around meat. Make roux with butter and flour. Pour on hot stock and stir until smooth. Add other ingredients to sauce. Adjust seasoning, simmer for 5 minutes, add cream and serve.

Boiled Fresh Tongue and Parsley Sauce

1 fresh tongue
1 bunch herbs
Salt

Cover tongue with cold water. Bring to boil and put in bunch of herbs and salt. Simmer gently for 3 - 4 hours. Take out and skin. Carve in slices and serve with parsley sauce and boiled cabbage.

Parsley Sauce
1½ oz butter, 1 oz flour, ¾ pint milk
1 small onion, ½ carrot, 1 stick of celery
1 bay leaf, 1 blade of mace, 6 peppercorns, salt
Infuse milk with vegetables and flavourings over gentle heat for 20 minutes. Melt butter and stir in flour. Add little by little the flavoured milk, stirring all the time. When smooth and of a good consistency add chopped parsley and seasoning. Simmer for another few minutes.

Aberdeenshire Meat Roll

1 lb minced raw steak
4 oz bacon, finely chopped
4 oz white breadcrumbs
1 medium onion, finely chopped
1 egg, beaten

Chopped parsley
Salt and pepper
Browned breadcrumbs

Mix all ingredients, season well and bind with beaten egg.
Put into well-greased meat roll jar. Put cloth or greaseproof paper over top and tie. Stand in saucepan with
boiling water and steam for about 1½ hours. Cool slightly
and turn upside down on to plate. When cold, coat with
browned crumbs and serve sliced with salads.

Roast Guinea Fowl with Oatmeal Stuffing

1 guinea fowl
2 rashers fat bacon
2 oz butter
Salt and pepper

Oatmeal stuffing
1 cup shredded suet
1 cup oatmeal
1 egg, beaten
Chopped parsley, salt and pepper

Butter guinea fowl all over with softened butter. Make stuffing by mixing all the ingredients and binding with beaten egg. Put in stuffing and cover breast with bacon. Season and roast for about 1 hour basting frequently. Add stock made with giblets to juices in the pan to make gravy. Serve with bread sauce and roast potatoes.

Meat Pasties

12 oz of left-overs of roast beef or lamb, minced
8 oz mashed potatoes
1 teaspoon chopped parsley
Grating of nutmeg
Salt and pepper
1 – 2 eggs, beaten
Browned breadcrumbs

Mix meat, potatoes, parsley and seasoning. Add enough beaten egg to bind. Shape into cakes about ½ inch thick on floured board. Dip into beaten egg and then cover all over with browned crumbs. Fry on both sides. Drain on kitchen paper and serve with hot gravy separately.

Boiled Chicken with Rice and Cream Sauce

1 large chicken
3 onions
4 carrots
3 leeks
1 bay leaf
1 bunch of parsley stalks
1 sprig of thyme
1½ oz butter
1½ oz flour
8 oz rice
¼ pint cream or top of the milk
Salt and pepper

Put chicken in large pan with vegetables, herbs and seasoning. Almost cover with water and bring to the boil. Simmer for 1½ hours. Lift out chicken and vegetables and keep warm. Strain stock and return to boil. Throw in rice and cook for 15 - 20 minutes. Drain rice, keep warm, reserving stock. Melt butter and make roux with flour and then pour on about ½ pint of the strained stock. Stir and simmer for a few minutes until hot and smooth. Add cream, chopped parsley and adjust seasoning.

Carve the chicken into joints and pieces, removing skin and place in the middle of ashet. Arrange vegetables and rice in a border around chicken. Mask chicken with some of the sauce and serve the rest separately. The remainder of the stock will make a delicious chicken broth for another day.

Chicken, Ham and Egg Pie

This dish can be made with left over chicken and stock from the previous recipe.

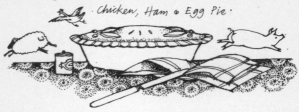

Chicken, Ham & Egg Pie

1 chicken
½ lb cooked gammon
3 hard-boiled eggs, quartered
1 tablespoon chopped parsley
1 dessertspoon chopped mixed herbs
1½ oz butter, 1½ oz flour
¾ pint stock, a little cream, a squeeze of lemon juice
Salt and freshly ground black pepper
Puff pastry
1 egg beaten with a pinch of salt

Poach chicken in boiling water with vegetables for about 1 hour. When cold, skin and carve into pieces, not too small. Cut gammon into thick strips. Melt butter and make roux with flour. Pour on ¾ pint liquid from chicken stock and stir until smooth and still quite thick. Season, add squeeze of lemon juice and cream. Put layer of chicken into bottom of pie dish, then some ham and quartered hard-boiled eggs. Season well and scatter over chopped parsley and mixed herbs. Spoon over a little of the sauce to cover. Continue until pie dish is full. Put eggcup upside down in centre to keep pastry up. Finish off with a good covering of the sauce.

Cover pie dish with pastry, pinch edges and "knock up". Decorate with leaves and make three or four ½ inch slits near centre. Brush all over with beaten egg and salt. Place in hot oven and cook for about 1 hour until pastry is golden and well-risen.

Pot Roast "Bubbly Jock"

Locally, roast turkey is still referred to as "Roastit Bubbly Jock".

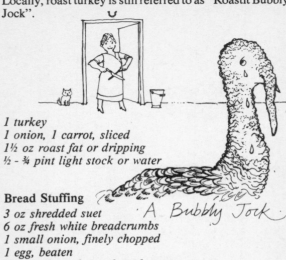

A Bubbly Jock

1 turkey
1 onion, 1 carrot, sliced
1½ oz roast fat or dripping
½ - ¾ pint light stock or water

Bread Stuffing
3 oz shredded suet
6 oz fresh white breadcrumbs
1 small onion, finely chopped
1 egg, beaten
Chopped parsley, salt and pepper

Mix all dry ingredients for bread stuffing and bind with beaten egg. Stuff turkey and sew up. Melt roast fat or dripping and when hot, brown turkey all over. Add vegetables and brown a little. Season and add stock. Cover and cook slowly for 2 - 2½ hours, turning and basting from time to time. Lift out turkey and vegetables. Strain stock and skim off fat. Reheat stock in saucepan and thicken slightly with kneaded butter and flour or a little cornflour. Carve turkey and serve gravy separately.

Running Away Bubbly Jocks.

Seven Cup Pudding

A cup of each of the following:
Fresh white breadcrumbs
Self-raising flour
Brown sugar
Shredded suet
Currants
Raisins
2 beaten eggs topped up with milk

1 teaspoon mixed spice,
Grated lemon rind
Golden syrup

· Seven Cup Pudding ·

Mix all dry ingredients. Mix with milk and eggs. Turn into buttered basin and cook as for previous recipe.

Cloutie Dumpling

For the uninitiated "cloutie" means cloth.

1 lb self-raising flour
12 oz raisins, 12 oz sultanas
4 oz butter or shredded suet
2 teaspoons cinnamon, 2 teaspoons mixed spice
6 oz caster sugar
2 eggs
¾ pint milk

Mix all ingredients with eggs and milk to make a soft mixture. Scald cloth and lightly flour on one side. Put mixture into floured side and tie up. Put a plate on bottom of pan and place dumpling on top. Fill up half way with boiling water and steam for 3 - 4 hours. Replenish with more boiling water from time to time.

Lemon Pudding

4 oz butter
4 oz sugar
4 oz fresh breadcrumbs
2 yolks of egg
Grated rind and juice of 2 lemons
½ teaspoon baking powder
Golden syrup

Cream butter and sugar and add eggs. Beat well and add breadcrumbs and lemon juice and rind. Add baking powder and turn into a buttered charlotte mould. Cover with buttered paper and steam for 45 minutes. Turn out and serve with some warmed syrup mixed with a little more lemon juice.

Syrup Sponge

8 oz self-raising flour
4 oz butter
4 oz sugar
2 eggs, beaten
2 - 3 tablespoons golden syrup
A little more syrup and a squeeze of lemon juice

Cream butter and sugar. Add beaten eggs and stir in flour. Grease pudding bowl and spread syrup over bottom and all round sides. Spoon in mixture and cover with buttered greaseproof paper. Tie and steam in boiling water for 1½ - 2 hours. Turn out on plate and serve with more syrup heated with a squeeze of lemon juice.

Baked Apples with Whisky Butter

1 large cooking apple per person
Cloves, dates, raisins, currants and sultanas
Lemon juice
Brown sugar
Butter

Baked Apples
with Whisky Butter

Whisky Butter

2 oz butter
2 oz soft brown sugar
2 tablespoons whisky (or drambuie)
A little grated lemon rind, a squeeze of lemon juice

Core apples and prick all over with fork. Fill hole with mixture of dried fruits, lemon juice and 1 clove each. Cover apples all over with softened butter and sprinkle with sugar. Bake for about 30 - 40 minutes in moderate oven. Cream butter thoroughly and beat in sugar by degrees with grated rind and juice of lemon. Add whisky gradually and then serve apples with a spoonful of the butter on top of each one.

FAVOURITE PUDDINGS

Bread and Butter Pudding

3 or 4 slices of bread, quartered
Sugar
A handful of sultanas and currants
1 egg
About ½ pint milk and a few drops of vanilla essence

Butter a pie dish and place pieces of buttered bread on bottom. Sprinkle on currants and sultanas and a little sugar. Continue layers to fill dish. Cover with egg and milk mixture. Sprinkle well with sugar and dot over with butter. Bake in moderate oven until custard is nearly set and the top well browned.

Custard Pudding

2 oz butter
3 oz sugar
Yolks of 2 eggs
½ pint milk
2 tablespoons plain flour
A few drops of vanilla essence
2 egg whites

Cream butter and sugar. Add yolks, flour and essence. Bring milk to boil and pour over mixture slowly. Stir over gentle heat until custard thickens. Pour into pie dish. Whip whites of egg with a little sugar and spread on top of custard. Brown in oven for a few minutes.

Eve's Pudding

1½ lbs apples, 2 tablespoons sugar
4 oz butter, 4 oz sugar, 4 oz self-raising flour
2 eggs

· Eve's Pudding·

Cook apples with sugar and a little water until tender. Place in a buttered pie dish. Cream butter and sugar until light. Beat in eggs one at a time, adding a little flour with each. Spoon this mixture over apples and bake in moderate oven for 30 minutes or until sponge is well risen and golden brown on top. Dust with icing sugar and serve with custard.

Treacle Tart

2 tablespoons brown breadcrumbs
2 - 3 tablespoons golden syrup
A little grated lemon rind and a squeeze of lemon juice
Sweetened shortcrust pastry

Line flan case with pastry. Mix breadcrumbs, syrup and lemon rind with juice. Fill pastry case and make a lattice of pastry strips on top. Bake in moderately hot oven for about 30 minutes. Serve with cream.

Apple Snow

1 lb apples
Whites of 4 eggs
Rind of 1 lemon
4 oz sugar

Peel, core and quarter apples. Put into pan with lemon peel and sufficient water just to prevent them from burning — about ¼ pint. When they are soft, take out peel and mash the apples to a thick pulp. Cool. Beat egg whites until quite stiff and frothy. Mix with apples and add sugar. Continue whisking until the mixture is still. Heap into glass dish or individual dishes and serve with cream.

Gooseberry and Elderflower Fool

1½ lb green gooseberries
A few heads of elderflower
½ pint water
4 - 6 oz sugar, according to taste
¼ pint custard
¼ pint lightly-whipped cream

Dissolve sugar in water and boil for 3 - 4 minutes. Put in gooseberries and simmer until tender. While cooking put in washed elderflowers tied in a muslin bag. Remove bag and drain gooseberries reserving a little syrup to thin purée if necessary. Sieve gooseberries and beat in custard. When quite cold add cream and pour into glass bowl or individual glass dishes. Serve with sponge fingers.

Jam Roly-Poly

Jam — raspberry is very good
8 oz self-raising flour
A little sugar
4 oz suet, shredded and cold water to mix

Sift flour and salt. Add suet and sugar. Rub in lightly and mix to a light dough with water. Roll out on floured board into a strip 7 - 8 inches wide. Spread with slightly warmed jam, not too near edge. Roll up and press edges together. Bake 30 – 40 minutes in moderate oven. Serve with custard.

Queen of Puddings.

Queen of Puddings

2 oz fresh white breadcrumbs
1 oz butter
1 oz caster sugar
2 eggs
Pared rind of a lemon
½ pint milk
3 tablespoons raspberry or strawberry jam
4 oz sugar for meringue

Infuse lemon rind in milk. Strain and add butter and sugar Stir until dissolved and add breadcrumbs. Add egg yolks and turn into buttered pie dish. Bake in moderate oven for 30 minutes. Cool and cover with jam. Whip egg whites until stiff and fold in sugar. Spoon on to top of pudding and sprinkle over with a little more sugar. Bake in slow oven until meringue is slightly browned.

Strawberry Shortcake

1 lb strawberries
4 oz flour
3 oz butter
1½ oz icing sugar
Vanilla essence
1 egg yolk
3 tablespoons redcurrant jelly
Whipped cream

Sift flour and sugar and make a well in centre. Add soft butter, egg yolk and vanilla essence. Work in together until a smooth paste. Set in a cool place for 30 minutes. Roll out into round ¼ inch thick and prick all over. Bake in moderate oven for about 20 minutes. When cool, cover with strawberries. Boil up redcurrant jelly and brush all over top of strawberries. When set pile over whipped cream.

Honeycomb Mould

2 eggs
1 pint milk
1 teaspoon vanilla essence
2 tablespoons caster sugar
½ oz powdered gelatine

Heat milk with gelatine gently until dissolved. Separate eggs and beat yolks with sugar. Pour over strained hot milk and stir over low heat until custard thickens. Add vanilla and cool. Whip egg whites stiffly and stir into custard. Pour into a mould rinsed out with cold water and leave in a cool place to set. Turn out.

A Burnt Cream

This pudding, although known as Cambridge Cream and Crème Brûlée in more recent times, allegedly originated from an Aberdeenshire country house recipe. Apparently the recipe was offered to the kitchens of Trinity College, Cambridge and "was rejected with contempt by an undergraduate". Some 30 years later it was presented again when the same undergraduate was a Fellow. He liked it this time and it became the favourite dish of May Week!

Cambridge & Crème Brulée

4 egg yolks, 1 pint cream, caster sugar

Beat eggs in basin. Heat cream and when boiling pour it on to the yolks, stirring well. Return to pan and stir carefully over heat until it thickens well — do not allow to boil. Pour into shallow fire-proof dish and allow to stand for several hours or overnight. Cover the cream evenly with about ¼ inch layer of caster sugar. Put under hot grill and allow sugar to melt and turn light brown. Stand for 2 - 3 hours before serving. This is delicious in summer with a layer of freshly picked raspberries under the cream.

Worried

SOME SAVOURIES

Scotch Woodcock

Scotch Woodcock

Yolks of 4 eggs
4 slices toast without crusts
¼ pint double cream
Pounded anchovies or a little anchovy essence
Salt and pepper

Beat yolks slightly and add salt and pepper to taste. Add cream and cook in double saucepan until just a little thicker than double cream. Pour over well-buttered toasts on which a little anchovy has been spread. Serve at once.

Devilled Soft Herring Roes

½ lb soft herring roes, a little seasoned flour
Lemon juice, hot buttered toast
Salt, pepper and cayenne
1 oz butter

Roll roes lightly in seasoned flour. Heat butter in pan and put in roes. Season and brown on one side. Turn over, season again and brown. Squeeze a little lemon juice over the roes and serve at once on hot buttered toast.

Finnan Haddie Savoury

1 smoked haddock, cooked and flaked
A nut of butter, salt and pepper
1 egg, beaten
Browned breadcrumbs, sprigs of parsley

Pound fish and bind with butter and some of the beaten egg. Season highly. Shape into little balls, dip in beaten egg and roll in breadcrumbs. Fry in deep fat and serve with fried parsley.

Smokie Tartlets

1 Arbroath Smokie
¼ pint very thick seasoned white sauce
Chopped chives, a little cream, salt and pepper
Tiny pastry cases made with a cheese shortcrust

Flake smokie and mix with enough sauce to bind. Stir in chives, salt and pepper and a little cream. Fill into cooked pastry cases and put in hot oven for 10 minutes.

Cod's Roe

Cod's roe
A little seasoned flour
1 egg beaten, seasoned flour
Browned breadcrumbs
Triangles or crescents of fried bread

Slice boiled cod's roe and cover with a little seasoned flour. Dip in beaten egg and roll thinly in breadcrumbs. Fry on both sides until brown and serve on dish mixed with croûtons.

Devils on Horseback

2 prunes per person, 1 bayleaf, a little red wine or water
Almonds, anchovy fillets, ½ rasher bacon each prune
Freshly ground black pepper, cayenne
Fingers of hot buttered toast

Soak prunes in red wine or water for 30 minutes. Simmer
with a bay leaf until tender. Take out stone and stuff with
almond wrapped with an anchovy fillet. Wrap each prune
with bacon and grill or put on baking tray in hot oven for 5
minutes. Set each roll on a finger of hot buttered toast.
Sprinkle with pepper and cayenne and serve very hot.

Mushrooms on Toast

Field mushrooms, salt and freshly ground black pepper
Butter and strips of hot buttered toast 1 x 3 inches

Allow about 3 mushrooms per person. Fry gently in butter
and season. Arrange on hot buttered toast.

Cheese Straws

Cheese Straws

6 oz flour
3 oz butter
1 oz grated cheese
1 egg yolk
Salt, pepper and cayenne

Rub butter into flour lightly and add cheese and seasoning.
Bind with egg yolk and a little water if necessary. Roll out
and shape into rectangle. Cut into 2 inch strips and gather
in little bundles of 6 or 8 ringed round with another strip.
Lay them on a very lightly floured baking tin and bake for
5 - 7 minutes in a hot oven. Serve very hot, one bundle on
each plate. They will reheat perfectly.

Cockles and Bacon Savoury

Cockles
Lean bacon, grilled and cut in large pieces
A little seasoned flour
1 egg, beaten, browned breadcrumbs

Roll cockles lightly in seasoned flour. Dip in beaten egg
and then roll in breadcrumbs. Fry quickly turning until
nicely browned and crispy. Serve with bacon.

Cheese Soufflé

Cheese Soufflé

¼ pint cheese sauce made with 3 oz grated cheese
3 yolks and 4 whites of egg
Salt, cayenne and paprika pepper
Browned crumbs, some extra finely grated cheese

Butter a large soufflé dish and tie buttered paper round to project above the rim about 2 inches. Secure with a paper clip. Alternatively butter individual ramekin dishes. Beat the egg yolks one by one into the slightly cooled cheese sauce. Add salt and cayenne pepper to taste. Fold stiffly beaten egg whites carefully into mixture. Turn into prepared dish, two-thirds full and dust with browned crumbs. Bake in a moderately hot oven for about 20 minutes or 10 minutes for ramekins. Remove paper and serve immediately with extra cheese and paprika sprinkled over the top.

Kinharachie Croûtes

2 eggs, 2 oz grated cheese
Small rounds of fried bread spread with anchovy essence
4 olives

Beat eggs and cheese well. Stir in thick pan over heat until thick. Pour over each croûton a small quantity and put an olive in the middle.

COMING SOON!

Jamie Fleeman's book of

Hearty Breakfasts

and

High Teas